We Make Films!!!
A Young Filmmakers Handbook

By Brian Southers

A B-South Project

WE MAKE FILMS!!!, Copyright © 2011 by
B-South, Ltd.
All rights reserved. The publisher grants the original purchaser of this book the right to reprint portions of the book for classroom use. Otherwise, no part of this book may be reproduced in any form, except for brief reviews, without written permission of the publisher.
Printed in the United States of America.
For information, address 1933 E. Dublin-Granville Rd. #189, Columbus, Ohio 43229

3D Layout completed in Poser 8 using existing 3D models and 3D models from www.Daz3D.com.

Special thanks for editing the book:
Wendi Flores
Donnetta Peaks
Kelly Burton-Roberts
Kimberly White
www.b-south.com

ISBN: 978-0-692-01452-3

This book is dedicated to six of my senior students SeVaughn Collins, Brianna Flores, Wyatt Haines, Keigan Knowlton, Nick Miller and Jonathan Swigert. All six have impressed upon me the value of education and the need for constant modification of instructional implementation. I thank them. It has been a joy teaching them.

4

Table of Contents

Introduction - Who Should Read This Book	8
Chapter One – Starting With You	9
Your Value	9
Always Finish	11
Your Practice	11
Your Film	12
Chapter Two – The Story	14
Short on Ideas	16
Keep it Simple	16
Focus on the Details	17
Believability	17
Be Human	18
Story Conflict	19
Image Representation	20
Chapter Three – The Structure	23
The Idea	23
The Premise	23
The Research	24
The Treatment	24
The Outline	25
The Screenplay	26
Screenwriting Software	28
Chapter Four – Before You Film	30
The Rehearsal	30
Composition	31
Master Shot	33
Storyboard/Floor Plan	34
Shot List	36
Crew	36
Lock the Location	36
Attention to Lighting	37

Attention to Audio	37
Gather Props	38
Discuss Wardrobe	38
Perks for the Crew/Actors	39
Filming Day	39
Chapter Five – Breaking Bad Habits	41
Filming Without Organization	41
Zooming While Recording	42
Eyelevel	42
Handheld	43
Obsession with the Long Shot	43
Using the Auto Button	44
Operating the Camera	44
Chapter Six – Composition: "The Box"	46
Camera Movement	47
Placement –Rule of Thirds	48
Framing	49
Profile Shot	50
Over the Shoulder Shot	50
Reaction Shot	51
3D Space	51
Perspective	51
Foreground/Background Information	52
Screen Space	53
180-Degree Rule	53
Filming Ratios	55
Chapter Seven – The Camera	57
Focal Length	58
Light	60
Iris	60
F-Stop	61

White Balance	62
Really Bright Light	64
Neutral Density Filters	64
Really Dim Light	64
Gain	65
Shutter	65
Focus	67
Chapter Eight – Image Stabilizers	70
Tripod	70
Monopods	72
Other Support	72
Chapter Nine – Image Quality	73
Lens	73
Resolution	74
Frames Per Second	75
Fast/Slow Motion	76
Exhibition	76
Chapter Ten – Audio	78
Audio Meters	79
Audio Waveforms	79
Recording Ambience	81
Chapter Eleven – Putting it All Together	83
Filming Outside on a Sunny Day	84
Filming Outside on a Cloudy Day	85
Filming Outside at Night	86
Filming Inside a House	87
Filming Inside a School	88
Chapter Twelve – Editing	90
Back Up	91
Editing at the Same Resolution	91
Managing the Edit	91
Edit to Script & Storyboard	92

Editing out the Bad Stuff	93
Selecting the Best Material	93
Using Cuts Only	93
Matched Editing	93
Overlapping Editing (J Cut/L Cut)	94
Starting From Black/Ending In Black	94
Using Titles/Credits	95
Making Corrections	95
Chapter Thirteen – Soundtrack	97
Dialogue	97
Ambient Track	98
Sound Design	98
Effects	98
Score	98
Music	99
Chapter Fourteen – Exhibition	100
Exporting the Project	100
Project Exhibition	101
Social Networks	101
Online Video Providers	101
Chapter Fifteen – Closing Advice	103
Practice, Practice, Practice	103
Build Relationships	103
Learn More	104
Suggested Resources	105
Vocabulary	106

Who should read this book?

For the one who has made a few short films and realizes s/he needs a little help. For the one who has a creative inspiration, but no knowledge of what to do next. For the one who has some idea of how to proceed, but could use a guide along the way, this book is for you. Although it is geared toward teenagers, anyone wanting to learn the art of making a short film can get an enormous amount of information from this resource. This is a how-to book, but learning is now a cross–platform endeavor. Books can tie to websites, websites can connect to iPods and computer downloads, all making for an impactful and intense learning environment. Read this book, but also engage with the online assessment tools that will help to reinforce knowledge and understanding. One can read a book (or read many books) from cover to cover, but it is through assessment that we demonstrate how much information is ultimately retained.

Your online experience begins at B-South.com where you can take online quizzes, ask questions, and get answers. The goals are to be inspired, prepared and well-trained for your next project. Filmmaking involves knowing an enormous amount of information about different aspects of technology, the story, and the mechanics of the equipment.

Before you start any process, it's a good idea to take a few quizzes and score well on them. If you do not score well, just take them again. Since learning is our only objective, there are no penalties for making errors. Powerful stories require powerful filmmakers and good filmmaking begins with a solid foundation. This book begins that process.

CHAPTER ONE
STARTING WITH YOU

YOUR VALUE

When you finish with this book, you should have a clearer understanding of how to write a better story, how to tell a story visually, and how to tell a story technically. These three objectives (tasks) are interwoven throughout this book so you are able to practice with this information over and over again.

The purpose of this book is to add to your value, meaning: You + This Book = More. I am using the word value in two different ways. The first way is to describe all the helpful information you have accumulated in your life up to this point. The second way is to describe how special you are as a person.

The first type of value you can think of is your power source. The more your value increases, the stronger your power source becomes. Think of it like a battery. Some batteries have more power than others. Making a film requires a good amount of power. It takes so much time and effort to write, produce, film, edit, and distribute a film that it is absolutely necessary to have a fully charged battery that will supply you enough power to complete your project.

Think of the second type of value as all that you are. Allow me to relate you to a container filled with many pieces and parts. These pieces and parts are what make the container special. This is true for you as well. Your value is why others need to see your creative films. People may have seen many action films, but not an action film made by you. They may have seen a million romance films, but not a love story told by you. As you make your film and you hit different roadblocks and setbacks, you must remind yourself that you are valuable and the audience deserves to witness your value through your film.

Remember, within the parameters of this book value has two meanings: who you are and what you do. To add to this, you are important to you and to others. What makes you so important is your ability or capacity to act (to do something) or more importantly, to contribute. So your value always brings about some type of action. The more you read, the more information you receive, which in turn empowers you to create a greater impact with your story. It's critical that you read all the chapters in this book.

A few months from now, you will be working on your film and will become frustrated. During this time of frustration someone might ask you, "Didn't you do your research?" You will confidently respond, "Yes, I did. I read a film book by B-South." The person may continue with another question, "How many pages did you read?" After pondering for a few moments, your eyebrows will raise and your eyes roll to the side as your

11

mind gathers all the memories related to reading this book. Then you'll slowly state, "I read about twenty or so pages." Suddenly it occurs to you that maybe reading a bit more would have helped you avoid this frustration.

ALWAYS FINISH

Finishing is important. It is neither the start nor the middle, but the finish that makes all the difference. This idea is not limited to reading a book or completing a film. It can be applied to everything else in your life. Even if you start life at a disadvantage, don't worry. As long as you obtain the goal, the rest of the baggage becomes unimportant. If you focus on your value, then everyone else is able to witness that value by what you do (your films) and accomplish, and how you comport yourself. Your value is directly tied to completion, meaning the more you complete, the more your value increases. It does not remain stagnant, and it definitely does not decrease. You can relate it to human growth. We do not decrease in age or lose childhood knowledge as we grow, rather, these values increase.

I want you to get information from this book, but I also want you to really understand it. So read on and read on well.

YOUR PRACTICE

There is a famous hip-hop artist was from the '80s, named Heavy D. In one of his songs he says, "perfectly I practice so I practice perfectly." Who says great knowledge can't come from the mouths of rappers? Heavy D makes two powerful statements. The first is practice. The second is practice correctly. You can practice making films every week and every week you can have a film full of errors. To avoid the errors, let's just get rid of them by correcting them. No film is perfect, but the more you practice *correctly*, the greater your impact will be on your audience.

Practicing allows you to reach certain goals. Some people practice enough to reach amateur status. Others practice more and thereby become hobbyists. Still, others practice even more to reach professionalism, and a select few practice to reach a master level of professionalism. My goal is to put you on the road to the master level. Why aim for anything less? Musicians practice everyday, dancers practice continuously and the same should be true for you. But let's start small. One film a week. That is, one short film lasting anywhere from ten seconds to 3 minutes. So what about the 20, 45 or even 90-minute film? We'll let you take a stab at those films when you work on your thesis in graduate school. When you perfectly practice with small steps first the big steps don't seem as big as they would. Every time you start a film remember the two P's – *Practice Perfectly*.

YOUR FILM

There is a caution statement found on precious packages to handle with care. The more precious the package, the more times you will find this message plastered everywhere. The same goes for making films; you must handle them with care.

Films are special, they can make people laugh, cry, think, and even make people believe, but to gain this control over your audience your film will require a good, solid story and a huge dose of creativity.

Spend enough time making your story as good as it can possibly be. After you finish, have someone read it. Your parents and friends are good to give input, but to get a nonbiased critique, find a teacher, professor, or some other adult.

THINKING QUESTIONS

1. What are two ways to describe value?

2. How would you describe your value?

3. Why is it important to always finish?

4. Why is it important to finish reading this book?

5. Why is it important to practice? What are a few ways practicing can benefit you?

CHAPTER TWO
THE STORY

Okay you have this great idea that has been brewing in your mind for a long time. You grab your camera, call up some friends and begin filming. Once you are done you begin the long process of editing. A few hours into editing you realize that your film suffers from many story problems. How could you have avoided these issues? It all starts with a good, solid story.

Some immediate problems you encounter: the helicopter that has to fly over the white house; a car crash that happens in the middle of a busy street with one thousand people; aliens that fall from the sky and sprout wings before they hit the ground. All of these scenarios are easy for Hollywood, but difficult for everyone else. Instead of going in this direction let's go in another. Let's say all you have available is a guitar, clothes, a basketball, some old football helmets and two siblings that will do almost anything for a Jolly Rancher and a trip to

McDonald's. In this case, your movie will only have all the items I just mentioned and two characters that are the same age as your siblings. This method is called **writing to your resources**. This means only write what is available to you. If your story is about an old man with a boat and your grandfather is three hundred miles away and renting a boat would cost $1,200 a day, this does not mean that you use your brother (who is fifteen) to act like your grandfather and substitute your go-kart for the boat. Instead, change the story to fit your brother with the go-kart. **Writing to your resources** is a very difficult concept for some to learn because filmmakers think they are giving up important parts of their story. Instead of focusing on what you do not have, recognize the value of all the resources available to you.

Once you know what resources you do have access to, then it is time to write that 20-minute story. These 20 minutes will take at least four or five days to film, and you will likely run into problems with your actors because they will not remember to wear the same clothes each day. So now your four-day project has increased to eight. A couple of those days, the weather was bad, so that extended your film to ten days. On day eight, two actors were not there because one became ill and the other had to go on vacation. Do you see where I am going? Long projects can have many more complications – complications that you can easily avoid with a shorter film. Ideally, you want to film in about four hours. This way the weather, actors and everything else remain consistent. How long should your film last? No more than **3 minutes** – *if* you can make your point in three minutes really well. It is easy to tell your story within a longer time span, but a well-executed 3-minute film can give the same results with your audience as a 5, 10 or 15-minute film.

16

Another difference between a **3-minute** film and any of the other longer versions is the greater amount of *quality* time you will have to spend on the 3-minute film. With longer films you will have to work faster. Working faster can cause more mistakes. So remember: 3 minutes.

SHORT ON IDEAS

What if you sit down to write and nothing comes out? You doodle on the page and begin typing period after period on the laptop until the entire page is filled. What do you do at this point? How do you proceed? You can spend minutes, hours, days or even months stuck, trying to move forward. If you ever get to this point, remember to build from others. Who are the others? The others are outside resources: that newspaper article, conversation you overheard at a grocery store, or the broadcast that was on the evening news. This is called inspiration. You are being inspired by an outside source. This outside source is that newspaper article, conversation, or news report. Then you build upon the inspiration to create a fictional story. The thing to remember about "being inspired" is to take what you heard or saw and craft a fictional story from it. Writing an exact story based from what you heard will in some way or form infringe upon someone's rights. Infringing on the rights of others can lead to their filing some type of legal action against you. We do not want that to happen, so we use information as inspiration, but do not attempt to copy and re-enact the events verbatim.

KEEP IT SIMPLE

Keep your story simple. Simple does not mean uninteresting. A simple story can still capture the hearts of the audience, but a complex story could leave the audience baffled trying to figure out its meaning. Complex story lines usually require more time to reveal all the important information. You do not have all of that time. Remember, your film is only 3 minutes, not a feature film, which is at least 90 minutes. An example of a simple story is a water boy running away from some football players. They gain on him, but before they can grab him he outsmarts them. A complex story is a water boy creates a mathematical equation that can systematically control the left side of a person's brain. He tries it out on some football players, but it is an utter failure.

FOCUS ON THE DETAILS

How do you keep a simple story interesting? **Focus on the details**. This is one of Donald Trump's signature statements. When he designs his hotels he focuses on small details. These details are what draw customers to his hotels and allow him to charge more. By paying attention to the smallest of details within your own story, you will also draw your audience closer to your film. If we pay attention to the details from the first story in the paragraph above, then we will not only focus on the boys running, but also reveal the cars rushing up and down the street, street lights changing, a crosswalk sign, cracks in the sidewalk, the boys' clothing flapping in the wind as they run, their sneakers, sweat coming out of their pores, the clinching of their fists, the grinding of their teeth, the on-lookers, the large buildings and the steam rising from the street vents. With every simple story there are hundreds of details that you can focus on to help enhance your story. Just remember to **Focus on the details**.

BELIEVABILITY

Okay, your story is short and simple, and you will focus on the details. What else is left? **Believability**. This means that if an actor is supposed to show fear, then he really looks scared. If an actor is playing a doctor examining a patient, the doctor must resemble what the audience believes a doctor to be. The examination room must resemble what the audience believes to be an examination room. Even though your story is fictional you are still representing the real world, real people and real emotions; this is why your story must maintain believability. Think of your story's believability as trust between you and your audience. At no time, under no circumstances can the trust be broken between you (your story) and the audience. If for any reason the audience does not believe that a prop is real or an actor's dialogue makes sense, a crack can form in the trust. Once a crack develops, it is almost impossible to repair. It's best to fortify your story and keep it impervious to cracks. Always keep the trust. Always maintain **believability**.

BE HUMAN

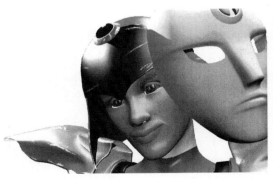

One way to boost your film's believability is to show **human subtleties**. If this seems a little abstract, let me explain further. Showing human subtleties is different from showing a scene's details because human subtleties focus on the character, whereas details include what is in the scene, in addition to the characters. Human subtleties are what make characters unique. They show the way a character's nostrils flare as he speaks, the way another character might raise one eyebrow higher than the other, or how a character fiddles with a pencil. These subtleties go beyond regular body movements into deeper human movements. Human subtleties do not show a person putting on a coat, but they show *how* a person puts on a coat. Is the coat put on neatly, quickly, rudely or even crazily? These subtleties are also very helpful for actors to understand how to portray their characters. So it is very important to select certain human subtleties carefully.

Now it is time to start writing the story. If any school subject is beneficial to you right now, it is English. What have those classes taught you? They have taught you that stories have a **beginning, middle, and an end**. The beginning is the introduction – where your characters are introduced and the conflict is defined. The middle is the struggle between the characters as the story heads toward a climax. The end is the resolution of the climax, which is also the solution to the conflict that began during the introduction. *Focus your attention on the middle.* Usually audiences know the beginning and the ending from the genre, marketing commercials and trailers, but what they don't know is how the middle unfolds. The twists and turns are what make the film worth watching and are ultimately what keep students tied to their seats.

STORY CONFLICT

A short story requires that the **conflict** be introduced quickly. Within a 3-minute story you have to reveal the conflict before the first 30 seconds are up. If a commercial can state a problem

20

and resolution in 30 seconds, then you can certainly introduce your conflict. The conflict is the problem that affects your main character (protagonist). The antagonist causes the problem that affects the protagonist. The antagonist is usually another character, but nature makes for a good antagonist as well. Think of the antagonist as the opposition to the protagonist. The conflict continues throughout the middle of the story moving toward the climax. When it seems as though all odds are against the protagonist, he or she becomes victorious. Remember, since you are telling a short story, it is imperative to get to the **conflict** very quickly.

When you watch a theater production what do you hear the most? If you said the actors speaking, you are correct. In theater, the dialogue drives the play, but this is not the case in film. The dialogue does not drive the story, but is part of the story. The dialogue aids the story like a necessary piece to the puzzle, but it is not the entire puzzle. Try to manage your dialogue so that it is only a part of the images and sounds of the story.

IMAGE REPRESENTATION

If the dialogue should not dominate your story, what should? The answer is simple: the images. There is a saying that if you want a film that just talks, get into radio. Images drive stories in films. Anything in your story that an image can represent or portray should be portrayed or represented by that image. As the saying goes, an image is worth a thousand words. The question is how do you go about it? How do you represent a story with images?

First, start with the images that come to mind as you think about your film. What do you see? What does the camera gradually reveal? What does the camera immediately show? Second, think about the relationship within the scene. Is it between two people, a mother and child, a father and his car or a family and a funeral? Let's say that it's between a family and a funeral. Let's show the following images.

1. Dark clouds rolling through the sky with no sun
2. Streets are empty
3. An open newspaper hovers down the sidewalk
4. A house sits between two other houses
5. Pictures are on the walls revealing a happy family of five
6. In the kitchen there are placemats for only four
7. A neighborhood park is empty, but the swings are slightly moving
8. A young man that was in the picture from the house sits on a Merry-Go-Round as it slowly rotates
9. Tree branches are swaying in the wind
10. A church parking lot is filled with cars
11. A church building hums with MUSIC – Not sure why this is in all caps
12. One by one hands touch a casket
13. Flower pedals fall to the floor
14. Decorated flower stands flood the area around the casket
15. The podium microphone shines from a momentary ray of sunlight coming from the stained glass windows
16. A mother steps close to the microphone, her lips almost touching
17. The sanctuary is filled with people

22

These are the images that would begin the scene.

As you can see there are many images to set the tone of the scene, and I was able to use images that helped connect a family and a funeral. Images are wonderful to work with and what is so great about working with images is that no two people will approach them the same way. One person will use a certain number and type of images, whereas another person will use a completely different set of images.

THINKING QUESTIONS

1. Give a couple reasons why it is important to write to your resources.

2. Where is some material you can use to get inspiration?

3. What are three ways that your story can maintain believability?

4. Why is it important to have human subtleties?

5. Is it important to communicate to the audience mainly with dialogue or with images? Why?

CHAPTER THREE
THE STRUCTURE

THE IDEA

The previous chapter outlined what goes into a screenplay. This chapter will discuss how to structure it. Everything begins with an idea. The house you live in, the car you ride in, the building you walk through, they all began as an idea in someone's head and so did your story. It began with an idea in your head and now we need to develop that idea into a story.

THE PREMISE

Before we can begin writing more details about your story we need a starting point and an ending point. Once we know where to begin and where to end, we can fill in the middle. Write your story in three to four sentences. It just needs to state the conflict and how the conflict is resolved.

24
THE RESEARCH

Those history classes you have dedicated yourself to for years will have prepared you to do research for your project. The term research might sound too much like school for you so let's swap that word out for **intel**. Intel is just a techie word for gathering information. You have information about your story and gathering intel will only make your story more powerful, believable and impactful. Gathering necessary intel does not need to be long or drawn out. Gather at least ten facts from the Internet that will help you tell your story or clear up areas that are obscure. Look for facts centered on your locations, characters, the characters' problems, wardrobe, props or anything else. Next, find one or two books you can skim through to help strengthen the facts you provide in the story. Lastly, talk to at least three people that can give you input, insight and additional knowledge about the different subjects, characters and locations in your story. Remember the acronym B.I.P., which stands for Books, Internet and People.

THE TREATMENT I

Once the premise is written the next step is to elaborate on those three to four sentences. Expanding them into large paragraphs or even pages. You want to provide every little detail, scene, character and the complete flow of the story. The writing follows a story format. Dialogue is not necessarily included, but any and all character action is provided. Feel free to write more than what you need. Having an abundance of information helps give you a good cache of material to work with when writing the screenplay. All the writing is in the present tense so watch your verb tense. This type of writing is called a treatment. A 3-minute film will have a treatment of one, single-spaced page. No double spacing – well you can, but then write two pages instead of one.

Last note: once your have finished your treatment, check it for spelling and grammatical errors. Then find two or three individuals who will give their honest feedback on your story. Take their input into consideration and make the necessary changes.

THE TREATMENT II

There is a second type of treatment. I write about this more for you to know that it exists than for you to use it right now. Later, when you are writing feature length films and a film executive wants to understand your story fully, they will request a treatment from you. This treatment is a complete telling of your story, but within all the details of every scene. The reader will have a clearer understanding of what the story is about than what a synopsis provides, but without reading the screenplay. Now we are going to use treatment I and save treatment II for a much later time.

THE OUTLINE

I personally find it helpful to use an outline between writing my treatment and screenplay. The outline is scene driven and will give you a snapshot of the narrative flow of your story.

Review this sample:

1. Neighborhood sidewalk
   a. Jack runs down the sidewalk holding his eye.

26

    b. Jack's mother drives beside him questioning his behavior.

2. Jack's House - Bathroom

    a. Jack sits on the floor as his mom applies some ointment to a bruise around his eye.

    b. A girl's toy falls out of his pocket.

    c. His mom asks if he has been stealing again.

    d. Jack looks out the window and sees a girl playing with her Barbie dolls. Her knuckles are bruised.

Lines #1 and #2 are where the action is taking place. Line #1 location is in the neighborhood. Line #2 location is in a residential bathroom. Under each location is the action for that location. As you can see it is straightforward and understandable.

THE SCREENPLAY

Just like a treatment, a screenplay is written in the present tense. With a screenplay you can only write what the audience can see and hear. You cannot put a character's thoughts into the screenplay because thoughts are not seen. If you create visuals for a person's thoughts you have successfully provided a way for the audience to see into a person's mind.

There is really only one basic rule to remember when writing the screenplay. *Always write within the structure.* Screenplays have structure because a successful production relies on a well-structured screenplay. This is similar to a successful floor, which are the vital ingredients for a marvelous building. The structure has three basic parts: A part to name the location, a part to provide all action, and a part for the dialogue. The part to name the location is called the **SCENE HEADING** and it is always written in capital letters. The SCENE HEADING starts the scene.

SCENE HEADING   **EXT. HOUSE – DAY**

The EXT. stands for exterior and means that the location will take place outside. There are only two designations for a location – EXT. or INT. You probably have already guessed that the INT. is an abbreviation for interior. The word at the end of the SCENE HEADING is "DAY." It tells us if the scene will take place during the day or night. If the scene is at night you would type "NIGHT." Just like there are only two designations for location there are only two designations to state time – DAY or NIGHT. If you noticed I skipped over explaining what "HOUSE" meant, because I wanted you to understand the two sections with little change. The area between them can vary dramatically because it states where the location is, which could be a house, garage, grocery store, attic, park, building, tunnel, etc. You can even type "HOUSE BATHROOM" meaning the scene will take place inside of a house bathroom, which is different than a bathroom at an amusement park.

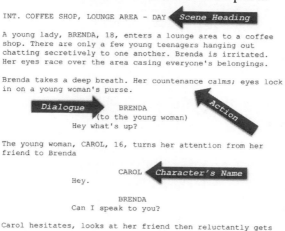

ACTION

The part of the screenplay that provides all the action is called "ACTION." Anything that is NOT dialogue is action. Describe the location in the action. Put all character movement, interaction and emotion in the action. All noises and sounds that you want the audience to hear should be typed in all capital letters. This way your editor will know what type of sounds you will need and where to put them. The first time a character is introduced, write their name in all capital letters. Afterwards it is not necessary. The reason for this is to inform actors when their character begins. Printing their name in capital letters makes it easy for them to spot.

DIALOGUE

The dialogue is what a character says. The goal is not to overuse the dialogue. If you can show it to the audience versus saying it then you should show it. It is best to keep the dialogue short and simple. To improve writing dialogue, start paying attention to how people speak.

THE REWRITE

After you have written your screenplay, it is called a First Draft. At this point, you need a few people to read it and provide input. Usually, someone can help you spot areas for improvement. Use the critiques to help you write a Second Draft. The Second Draft can go quickly because the bulk of your work is already done. No screenplay is perfect so you don't want to obsess over it, but you want to give your due diligence to fix any problem areas. Once you have completely finished, there is one thing left to do – check your grammar and your spelling. Your actors and crew will appreciate it.

SCREENWRITING SOFTWARE

Now start writing, but wait. It's helpful if I direct you to a free software program that you can download while you continue reading this book. Visit www.celtx.com and download their screenwriting software program. It is compatible with Mac and PC platforms. It is a complete software package for filmmakers that also includes areas for storyboarding and drawing floor plans. If you like to keep your writing online, then take a look at www.scriptbuddy.com. This service is also free to use but a paid subscription is required for the pro version (this is true up to the date of publishing this book, but verify all costs on their website). What is unique to www.scriptbuddy.com is the online feedback that you can receive within the community section of the website. This allows for invaluable critiques that often spot errors within your story you may have missed.

THINKING QUESTIONS

1. How is the premise different from the treatment and how is the treatment different from the screenplay?

2. How can your story benefit from research?

3. What are the definitions for a screenplay's scene heading, action and dialogue?

CHAPTER FOUR
BEFORE YOU FILM

THE REHEARSAL

The screenplay is finished. Your story is good. You did a couple of rewrites, added a few things and removed a few things away. Your format is solid. All spelling and grammar is great. So now you are ready to film. Well not quite, but we are close.

What can help you get a better performance from your actors before you film them? How can you know their idiosyncrasies and mannerisms? You might think you know your friend, but your friend that is playing a role in your film is an entirely different person. This is why rehearsals were invented. The **rehearsal** is the platform where you can visually see your actors play the roles for your film. What you dislike, you can change or get rid of all together. What you like, you can encourage, and expose different character behaviors. Why are you able to do this? That is the magic of the rehearsal. There is no pressure to get through the takes because you are losing light. There is no pressure to rush the actors because you will not have the location for long. The rehearsal is that magic time to take your screenplay and breathe life into it without all the other technical frustrations that come with filming.

For your 3-minute movie you need at least one 2-hour rehearsal. If you can rehearse at the location where you will film, even better. To begin the rehearsal, have everyone seat themselves in a circle or around a table and read the parts straight from the screenplay. Have a non-actor read all the action. Don't read anything but watch, listen and scribble notes on the side of the screenplay as the reading progresses.

After the reading is complete allow the actors to give input. Give consideration and recognize the value of their opinions. Next, you can walk them through the scene giving them instructions and showing them what you want from them at certain points of the story. Then have the actors act out the scene with or without the screenplay. If they are familiar with the material, then they can go without the screenplay and one of the non-actors can feed them their lines if they forget. At the end of the rehearsal, you should feel good because you have just saved yourself an enormous amount of time on the day of filming.

COMPOSITION

To alleviate the mystery, problems or decisions of setting the best shots, always ask yourself, "If I set the camera here what would it reveal, tell or show to the audience." When you set a shot you are allowing the audience to identify with your story. Maybe you want the audience to see much of your scene.

32

Maybe you want the audience to see a little. It depends on how you want the audience to relate to the story. The best way to learn **composition** and to help create shots for your own story is to watch a series of TV show episodes. Many episodes are available online at network websites (ABC, NBC, CBS, FOX, the WB, etc.), and are also available through paid subscription services (Netflix, Blockbuster, etc.). Within a few hours you can watch several episodes with the click of your mouse. Pay close attention to where the director is placing the camera. Instead of searching for a series or scene to match yours, just watch several episodes. BUT, what I want you to do is pull out a notepad and turn it sideways, then create five columns. The first column is the type of scene, the second is what the camera shows at the beginning, the third is whether or not the actors move, the fourth is whether or not the camera moves and the fifth is what the camera shows at the end. Create about ten rows, and for each column, describe to the best of your ability what is happening. Off to the side of the last column sketch out the floor plan for the camera and actors.

Sample:

	Scene Type	Camera Begin	Actor Move	Camera Move	Camera End

1.	Garage	Shows toolbox	Actor walks into frame with a wrench in hand. Another actor is working in the background.	Camera pans across the garage.	Camera pans to a grease spot on the car tire spokes.

There are many good episodes to use, but one show I prefer is *Law and Order*. Any of these episodes offer great examples of interesting scene composition. They usually have basic but powerful camera set-ups and very interesting actor movement. Pay special attention to what is in the **foreground,** or close to the camera, and what is in the **background,** or further away from the camera.

MASTER SHOT

There are many types of shots, but one of the most important is your master shot. Your **master shot** films the duration of the scene, but does not necessarily include all the content. If your scene is one minute and it has five trees and one boy in the scene, then your master shot is one minute long. Does the master shot need to show all the trees and the boy at once? No, the master shot can reveal portions of the trees and the boy. What is important to remember is the message of the scene must get through to the audience. Your intended message, whatever it may be, will dictate what is shown by the master shot.

When you are constructing your storyboard and floor plan, first concentrate on the master shot. Then move on to smaller shots (that is, shorter in duration, not short in size) that will help to draw your audience's attention closer to your message.

34

Remember to move your actors around. This is very helpful for an effective master shot. Maybe the actor starts far from the camera (Long Shot/Wide Shot or LS/WS) then walks very close to the camera (Close Up or CU). Maybe the two actors change positions. Maybe one actor turns away from another, thereby turning toward the camera. There are many directions you can go and it is probably easier to move the actors around than the camera. Just remember, if you decide to move your actors you must have a reason.

STORYBOARD/FLOOR PLAN
1.1 MEDIUM:

Ninja lurks in the shadow awaiting his enemy.

Another timesaver is setting up your camera ahead of time. This is called creating storyboards and a floor plan. You can do this before, during or after rehearsals; whatever works best for you. If you don't know how to draw, well I can't either. Just use a small still camera and take pictures of your intended shots. You can use the still camera in the same way large production companies use director finders, which is basically a zoom lens with an eyepiece. The director finder allows you to view the scene at different focal lengths before camera set up. Move around within your location to discover the best position for your camera.

The image at the top of the previous page is a sample of a storyboard. I used a 3D program to create the image. The image below the storyboard is a sample of the floor plan that shows where the Ninja, tree and camera are located. There is also additional information about the location of the lights. Both of these images were created with the free Celtx program that is available from their website www.celtx.com.

If you are building your storyboard prior to the rehearsal, then bring along a few friends or family to represent the characters within your story. Any person standing in for the actor is called a **Stand In**. If you set your storyboards during rehearsal, there is no need for Stand Ins. This does, however, add to your plate because the main objective of the rehearsal is not to create storyboards but to observe actor performance. Once you have finished taking all the pictures you can import them into the software.

The floor plan works directly with the storyboard. The storyboard shows what the camera sees, but the floor plan

36

shows where the camera is located and any change in camera movement.

Some would say that the storyboards and floor plans help to communicate your ideas to the crew, but even more importantly, the storyboards and floor plans help to communicate your ideas to yourself. This entire process is called pre-visualization.

SHOT LIST

After you have completed the storyboards you can arrange them in a sequential order. This way you can mark off the shots as you complete them. This is called the **Shot List**.

CREW

Who do you need? How many people do you need? Who can you do without? For your type of project the actors are responsible for their own wardrobe, hair and makeup. So that eliminates the **crew** persons for hair, makeup and wardrobe. You can have one person working the lights (if any) and the boom microphone (if any). One person you can never do without is the camera operator, and that person is probably you. You should have at least three people working behind the camera. The camera operator, audio and a production manager are all must haves. The production manager's function is complex, but on a simple set, the production manager (PM) will keep you on task, watch the time, get the actors situated and be the liaison between you and the rest of the world. Are they necessary? You bet they are. So now would be an ideal time to recruit your mother.

LOCK THE LOCATION

How do you make your filming day less stressful? **Lock your location** down. What does this mean? It means that you must gain full control of your surroundings. For example, if you are filming in your own house you might have to give your sister a few bucks to catch a movie with her friends so she is not making unnecessary noise yapping on the phone. You can make sure that you inform your parents about all the rooms you will need so they can make necessary preparations. If you are filming just outside your home, it is imperative that you notify all parties involved with the location so the police or a possible nasty neighbor will not cause unnecessary problems for you.

ATTENTION TO LIGHTING

Without light the camera cannot record an image, therefore, lighting is very important. The best approach is to start with a main light source. After you identify your main light source, you can build on it to light your scene properly. Could you use a window as your main light source? Could you use a lamp? What about light from a small desk lamp or light from the fluorescent overheads at a grocery store? If you are using a house, you may have to open the curtains to all the windows to allow enough light to enter the room. Then you can film at a right angle to the window.

A good reflector can go along way. It allows you to reflect your existing light onto your subject or actors. You can make one out of aluminum foil and wrap it around a foam core. You can purchase a 20x30 poster size foam core from your local business/paper supply company. You can also purchase

38

collapsible disk reflectors from any photography store. They are very handy and you can use them over and over again. I have some that are ten years old. Collapsible disk reflectors also have two sides to use as a reflector. They come in any combination of gold, silver or white.

ATTENTION TO AUDIO

Recording good audio is very important and we will discuss it in detail in a later chapter, but for now, I want to make you aware of all the necessary steps to take to achieve audio success. Go to your location, close your eyes and listen. What do you hear? Is it a dog that barks continuously from the neighbor's yard? Is it the refrigerator that you cannot turn off? Is it squeaky wooden floors that create an awful sound as you shift your weight? All of these are factors you must pay attention to. If not, you will discover how much they have affected your film when you sit down to edit.

You might need to choose another location because there are too many unwanted sounds, noises and vibrations in the area. Maybe the sound of the refrigerator is interfering in your scene. Perhaps you can unplug it and keep it closed. The coolness within should last a few hours, but check with your parents.

Keep all windows and doors shut to keep out traffic noise and intermittent wind noise from outside. If the floor is a problem, have everyone take off their shoes, or put a couple of covers down to muffle or dampen the vibration of sounds. If an actor is speaking, always have a microphone no more than one foot away. If your camera microphone is the only microphone you have, then you have to maneuver your actors close to the camera before they begin speaking.

GATHER PROPS

Your screenplay calls for a red cap, but on filming day, it is nowhere to be found. That's because no one brought it. Gathering **props** is an important task that can start days or even weeks before filming begins. Just like your shot list, create a prop list to keep a record of every item you need to borrow or purchase.

DISCUSS WARDROBE

Even though the actors are providing their own **makeup** and **wardrobe**, they still need a little direction on what clothes to wear on the set and what other clothes to bring. The clothes should fit the ambience and mood of the scene and help deliver your message to the audience. Once you finish filming, take a picture of the characters' clothes. If for some reason you have to come back to that particular scene, the actor can match the look they previously had in the scene.

PERKS FOR THE CREW/ACTORS

Feeding the actors and crew a good meal is a very useful perk. The time they spend can be long and demanding, so the $2 per person you might spend on them will go a long way. You need to do a little more than a bag of chips and a can of pop, but you do not have to give a four-course meal either. Just feed them well. That might mean buying a couple of boxes of good pizza or double stack hamburgers.

FILMING DAY

A lot of work was completed in order to prepare you for a successful film day. On that day, make sure you are on the set at least one hour early. If you are old enough to drink coffee, get yourself one and sip on it slowly. To set the tone for the day, start quickly with a simple shot then move on to your master shot. Your simple shot could show your actor walking through the door, stepping out of a car, tying his or her shoe, etc. Keep it simple. Once you have one in the bag, it is much easier to start the next one.

THINKING QUESTIONS

1. Why is it important to conduct rehearsals?

2. Describe how to manage a film rehearsal.

3. How can you improve your composition?

4. What is a Master Shot? Does it cover the entire length of the film or just one part of it?

5. What perks should you have for the crew and actors and why?

6. What should you take note of at a location in order to record good audio?

7. Why is it important to lock the location?

CHAPTER FIVE
BREAKING BAD HABITS

Thanks to consumer video cameras, buyers have developed a few bad habits (Maybe that is being a little harsh. Let me try again). Thanks to the access to consumer video cameras, users have developed a few bad habits. This is due to what I will call the **convenience factor**. The convenience factor is using camera techniques and functions to benefit the camera operator versus using those techniques and function to serve the creative process of the story.

FILMING WITHOUT ORGANIZATION

If you have a camera in your hand, what is holding you back from running outside and filming a masterpiece? If we aim to create the best film possible, then it takes a little preparation. Most of the time when customers are purchasing cameras the intent is to capture a moment. That moment could consist of a birthday party, a track meet, or even a school play. These moments take no preparation. Just whip the camera out, set it on auto and go. You do not want to copy this same behavior when working with your first story. Leave that way of thinking for basketball games, gymnastics and piano recitals. Your story will take a good deal of organization in order for it to make an impact on its audience. Organization, organization, organization; you will thank me in the end.

ZOOMING WHILE RECORDING

This is used as a quick fix to magnify the image. Zooming is fine for consumer use, but if the intent is to bring the audience closer to the action, then the camera should move toward the action. When the image is magnified, this is called zooming and the camera is not moving at all. What is happening is the lens is moving through what are called focal lengths. As the lens moves through these focal lengths the distance between objects either increases or decreases, which is not a natural representation of moving away or towards someone or something. The best practice, if you want to maintain realism and allow the audience to feel that they're right in the middle of the action, is to move the camera.

EYELEVEL

There is an eyepiece on the video camera, which helps you see what the camera is recording. It's important to realize that if you keep the camera at **eyelevel**, then everything you record will have a height that equals the distance your eye is from the ground. Camera angles need to vary depending on the story. Sometimes the camera might better serve the story if it is one inch off the ground. Sometimes it is better to put the camera fifteen feet in the air. The story should dictate camera placement and not the physical height of the camera operator – that is, the distance from his or her eye to the ground. I have written all of this to make the point: do not put the camera at eyelevel all the time. Mix it up. Allow the story to reign supreme when it comes to setting the camera at various heights.

HANDHELD

If it were up to me all video cameras would automatically come with a tripod. I would even go so far as to permanently attach a tripod to certain video cameras. This would eliminate the need to hold the camera. In some instances holding the camera can serve the story, especially for edgy material. But in most other instances, a tripod or some other support is necessary.

OBSESSION WITH THE LONG SHOT

Our eyes have a wide range of view. This is due primarily to the fact that we have two eyes side by side, thereby giving a much wider area of coverage then if we just had one eye. Since we have a wide range of view, we naturally try to recreate it when operating a video camera. Usually, most information recorded is a close representation to what you would see normally with your eyes. The problem with this approach is that the audience does not know what to focus on, or what is important within the scene. This problem is solved by just moving the camera closer to the subject/object or by pausing the recording, zooming the lens closer, then by continuing to record again. What we have to realize is that even though our eyes have a wide range of view, our minds usually focus in on certain areas of the scene and ignore other areas. To help the audience

44

accomplish the same thing, just isolate the subject /object by moving the camera closer.

USING THE AUTO BUTTON

There are features on the camera that allow it to do everything. The problem is, the camera will automatically make fluctuations as the subject's distance changes and as the light changes.

Another problem occurs when the camera does not know what to focus on or which subject to use in order to balance the light. Let's say there is a tree close to the camera, but you want to record a deer about twenty feet away. When using the camera's auto focus, the camera does not know that the tree is not your main subject and will set its focus to the tree. Let's also say a person is standing in front of a white wall. When using the camera's auto setting the camera will adjust to the white wall because the white wall reflects more light to the camera than the person. When the camera does this, the person will record darker in the camera. This means the person is underexposed, which is usually considered an error. So, my advice is to turn off all the auto settings and adjust the camera manually. Never fear, I am getting ready to show you how.

OPERATING THE CAMERA

Getting a good image is primarily based on knowing where the camera controls are and what they can do. Most cameras that can rest on your shoulder generally have the camera controls in the same areas. Usually the cameras you have to hold in your hand have controls located in a variety of places. Sometimes they are not even located on the camera, but inside of the internal camera menu. That being said, it is best to get to know whatever camera you are using. Literally all video cameras have a manual somewhere on the Internet. If you do not own a hard copy, download one from the company's website and review it to understand the basic controls.

Video cameras range dramatically in price. They can cost from $49 to over $100,000, so choose one based on your budget or available access. If you have $500 then find the best $500 camera that is out there. Technology is changing fast and what is considered great this month is good next month and okay the following month. Most cameras will allow you to control the camera manually and this is what you want. The resolution and the lens are what define a quality camera. Both are equally important. Some cameras have a fixed lens, meaning the lens is permanently attached to the camera. Other cameras have an interchangeable lens, meaning the camera can accept different types of lenses.

THINKING QUESTIONS

1. What are five common bad habits?

2. Why is it important not to zoom while recording?

3. What benefits are there to setting the camera at different heights?

4. What benefits are there to setting the camera at eyelevel?

CHAPTER SIX
COMPOSITION: "THE BOX"

Now what does a box have to do with making movies? They have two important things in common. You can put stuff in a box and you can take stuff out. The camera's frame has the same function. Anything that is within the frame is recorded in the camera. Anything that is not within the frame is not recorded. You can control what is recorded by minimizing what is in the frame (taking things out) or by maximizing (putting things in). If there is something in the frame that is not related to the story, remove it. Like a picture on the wall, a toy on the shelf, or the loaf of bread that did not make its way back into the breadbox, make sure you pay attention to everything that is inside your frame. Take a count of everything if you're inclined (unless there are blades of grass). Start at one corner and sweep your eyes around the entire frame from corner to corner. This will help you to become aware of everything there.

CAMERA MOVEMENT

I suggest you focus on two camera movements for now: **the pan and the tilt,** and leave the rest to look forward to for later use in other films. The pan is moving the camera from left to right and the tilt is angling the camera up and down. Once you master these two movements learning dollies, cranes, jib arms, Dutch tilts, and all other camera movements will be easier. When you pan with movement, it's necessary to keep space in front of the action. This is called the person's (the action) walking space. To maintain a smooth camera

movement, start slowly then increase speed. As you come to the end of the movement, decrease speed. Rehearse every camera movement before filming. This will increase your success. If you have two to three hours left, then take a stab at another type of camera movement. I suggest doing a dolly move with a wheelchair or, if you have hard wood floors, then use a wheeled dolly.

PLACEMENT - Rule of Thirds

Rule	of Thirds	

Usually when someone uses the camera they automatically put the person's head in the middle of the screen. This leaves a large amount of room above the subject's head and empty space to the left and right of them. The best approach is to compose the frame. When you compose the frame you are arranging how the contents within the frame are displayed to the audience. It is like a person wearing a cool looking outfit. It is not the clothes per se, but how the clothes are arranged on the person. The better the clothes are arranged the more appealing the person is to their admirer. This is also true when arranging contents within a frame. The better the arrangement the more impactful it is to the audience.

So how do you go about arranging a frame? Well, it is good to know a couple rules to apply to achieve good composition. The first rule is called the **RULE OF THIRDS** and the second is **PERSPECTIVE**. The rule of thirds divides the frame into thirds both horizontally and vertically. It takes two equally spaced lines to divide the frame into thirds horizontally and two equally

spaced lines to divide the frame vertically. Instead of having your person in the center of the screen move them to the first vertical line or second vertical line. To maintain the best headroom place the person's eyes right on the top horizontal line. The rule of fifths is similar to the rule of thirds, but instead of two lines there are four.

FRAMING

The closer you move the camera toward the character(s) or objects, the more personal they become to the audience. The inverse is also true: the further you move the camera away from the character(s) or objects the less personal they are. Close framing includes extreme close ups (ECU), close ups (CU) and medium shots (MS). **Framing** that is farther away are longs shots or wide shots (LS or WS) and extreme longs shots or extreme wide shots (ELS or EWS).

To help the audience understand where the characters are located, it is best to establish the location (establishing shot or ES). If the scene is taking place inside of a house, establish the scene by filming the outside of the house first. If a scene is taking place in the street, establish the shot by filming a wide shot of the neighborhood. If you are on a rollercoaster, film the

50

amusement park. If you are in a store, film the shopping mall. If you are in an office, film the office building.

It is best not to end the frame at the actor's knees, because the person could appear amputated.

Avoid ending the frame at the talent's ankles, because the talent could appear as if they are standing in something versus just standing on the ground.

Besides the shot sizes listed above there are many types of shots. Lets look at two of them: the profile shot and the over-the-shoulder shot.

PROFILE SHOT

The type of shot or framing that shows characters from the side versus the front is called the **profile shot**. This type of shot is less personal than a shot that is in front of the character. A profile is good for covering the following:

1. Two or more people talking
2. Someone thinking
3. Someone looking out of a window
4. Someone walking
5. Someone running
6. Two or more people fighting

OVER THE SHOULDER SHOT

The type of shot or framing that is over the shoulder of one character and shows the face of another is called an **over-the-shoulder shot**. This type of shot puts the audience outside of the conversation. The audience is looking or peeking in, but is not a part of the conversation. This is good for secretive conversations between characters or scenes when keeping the audience at a distance is important.

It is a good idea to put the shoulder of the character nearest the camera out of focus. This way more attention is given to the other character. In order to do this you need to have quite a bit of space between the character who is farther away and the camera, so you can zoom in as close as you can.

REACTION SHOT

Another type of shot deals with filming important information and where to place the camera. It is critical to capture the characters' reactions. How a character is reacting is more important than the one speaking. Do not underestimate the power of the **reaction shot**. When in doubt spend adequate time capturing reactions from your characters.

3D SPACE

How do you represent 3D space on a 2D screen? Perspective, foreground information, and background information is how we do it. 3D space takes into account the Z-axis. The X and Y-axes are for 2D space, but by adding the Z-axis or depth, creates 3D space.

PERSPECTIVE

Every scene has some type of lines. Whether it is a hallway, sidewalk, building, house, walls, trees, etc. Instead of having the line perpendicular to the frame, shift the camera to the left or the right so that the line is at an angle or slanted. Put the camera at an angle to the sidewalk or at an angle to the street or trees or shoreline, etc. When the frame is perpendicular to the lines within the scene, it represents more of a 2D space. When the lines are not perpendicular, the scene represents more of a 3D space. When the space is 3D it is more interesting.

Perspective will also be revealed by how the characters move around in the scene. Having the characters walk toward the camera along an imaginary diagonal line will show perspective. From far away the character will appear small, but as the character moves closer s/he will appear larger in size. If you want to preserve 2D space, then the character will stay the same distance from the camera as she moves from one side of the frame to the other.

FOREGROUND/BACKGROUND INFORMATION

What is close to the camera and far away from it shows 3D space versus having the characters or objects at the same distance from the camera. 3D space is even more interesting. Instead of framing the character in a close up and resetting the camera to film another character in Long Shot, just frame one of the characters in the foreground and the other in the background. You can save time and give the audience an interesting shot all in one take. Look at the image above **with the tree and the ninja**. The tree is in the foreground and the ninja is in the background.

SCREEN SPACE

Once you know about the rule of thirds, then it is helpful to understand screen space. The rule of thirds helps you achieve screen space because it allows you to arrange the contents to deliver your message to the audience.

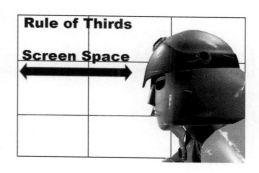

WALKING

If someone is walking leave space in front of the person to give them adequate space to walk. More space is in front of the person versus behind.

SPEAKING

If someone is speaking leave space in front of the person to give them speaking room. Also, the space in front is the space for the other characters.

LOOKING

If someone is looking in a certain direction leave space in front of them for them to look.

180-DEGREE RULE

Maintaining the placement of a person from one camera position to another is very important. Let's say you place person "A" on the left side of the screen talking to person "B" on the right side of the screen. Then you move the camera over to the right about ten feet and put the camera on the floor. Should person "A" be on the left side or the right? The audience will understand easier if person "A" remains on the left. Think of it as reading a book. On one page you have all the words typed left to right, but then on the other page the words are typed right to left. Think about how you would have to adjust to read the book. It is the same way with watching a film. If you want to throw the audience off or give them a sense of disorientation, then change the screen space for your characters. But if you want to allow the audience to read your scene easier, keep your characters' placement consistent from shot to shot.

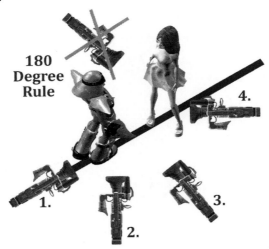

The above image shows four cameras. If camera number two was placed first it creates the line of action between the two actors. Camera positions three and four are both positions that obey the **180-Degree Rule**. Even though camera position number one is on the actual line it still obeys the rule.

What if we then move the camera from the right side of the line over to the left side? If we do this, the characters would automatically flip screen space. Person "A" is not on the left side anymore but the right. Person "B" is not on the right side, but the left. This is called breaking the 180-degree rule.

The first camera position creates an imaginary line from the camera to the characters. When we move the camera to the left or the right from the first camera position, we create an area of space. This area of space is 180-degrees, which is a half circle. Moving outside of the 180-degree area or half circle will automatically cause your characters to swap sides of the screen. Whoever is on the left is now on the right. Whoever is on the right is now on the left.

Is there a way to break the 180-Degree Rule without the audience knowing? Yes, in fact here are three examples:
1. Place the camera directly on the 180-Degree Line, film a take, then move the camera across the line.
2. A continuous camera move can cross the 180-Degree Line.
3. The character(s) can move.

As stated above, you might also want to intentionally break the 180 Degree Rule to state a message or communicate something of importance to the audience. Just remember before you begin breaking rules, learn them well and have a really good reason for breaking them.

FILMING RATIOS

Let's say you film your Master Shot and it's great, but you decide to film it again with a couple slight modifications. Change the acting performance or change your actors' movement or delivery just to give yourself some options in the editing room. By filming it again you have filmed a two to one ratio (2:1). It is best to know how much space there is to record before beginning. If you have 60 minutes of space to film a 3-minute project, then you can have a 20:1 ratio. You can film the same master shot 20 times or the entire 3-minute film from multiple angles 20 times. Usually three or four takes will do, but if you get into a situation where you have filmed nineteen takes and you still have at least two more angles, go buy more media.

THINKING QUESTIONS

1. How is using a box similar to a camera frame?

2. What is the 180-Degree Rule? How would you break it?

3. What is screen space? How would you use screen space as a person is walking?

4. If you have eight takes what is the shooting ratio?

5. Why is the reaction shot so important? How would you use the reaction shot within your film?

6. How is panning the camera different from tilting the camera?

CHAPTER SEVEN
THE CAMERA

There are basically two parts to the camera, but usually we recognize it as just one piece. The lens is the first part and the body is the second. Both parts work together to capture the image. All consumer cameras have fixed lenses, which are not removable. Some consumer and most professional

Lens

Camera Body

cameras have a removable lens. With many professional cameras, you can purchase the body without a lens, and some come with adapters whereby you can attach photography lenses.

LENS FOCAL LENGTH

When the camera zooms in or zooms out, the image is increasing or decreasing in magnification. The lens magnification is expressed in focal length numbers. Focal **length** numbers are expressed in millimeters (mm). Large focal length numbers are used for the telephoto lens or long lens. Think about the lens the professionals use for football games and basketball games. The sizes of those lenses are really big. This is due to the magnification. The greater the magnification is, the larger the lens, hence the size of a telescope.

Small focal length numbers are considered wide. A really small number will give you fish-eyed results. A fish-eyed-lens is so wide that edges of the image are distorted hence the name "fish-eye." A number that is in the middle is considered a normal lens because it is similar to the human eye. What's important to remember is that lenses with large focal length numbers will compress space. This is understandable because there is magnification involved. Objects that are ten feet apart will appear closer together than what they are in real life. Take the above image; it has a lens of 400mm. Now look at the image below. Same camera but now the lens is 25mm. For both images the distance is either compressed (above) or increased (below).

On the flip side, lenses with small focal length numbers will exaggerate space; meaning objects will appear further apart. On the side view mirror of most cars, there is a little warning at the bottom that reads, "Warning: Images in mirror are closer than they appear." Why is this? Because the side view mirror is a wide-angle mirror. The mirror exaggerates the space between your car and the car behind you.

If you move from one type of camera to another type of camera, you will find that a 50mm lens on one does not match the 50mm of another. Why is this? It's because the area of coverage is also dependent on the area of capture. All cameras have a capture area inside the camera. If camera one has a

60

smaller capture area than camera two, then a small focal length number for camera one will match a larger number for camera two. This is easier to understand if we apply some numbers. Let's use film to do so.

A film camera that accepts 16mm roll film has a lens with a focal length of 25mm this is the same as a film camera that accepts 35mm roll film with a 50mm lens. The capture area for the 16mm roll camera is 16mm and the capture area for the 35mm roll camera is 35mm.

LIGHT

Light is so fundamental to your image that most of the functions of a video camera are directly related to it. There are two parts of light that concern us: its intensity and color. Let's start with the light's intensity because we experience it everyday. When we wake up in the morning, the light is dim. Then you go into an area of the house where the light is bright and you have to squint your eyes because the light is too bright. The difference between the light in your dark room and the bright room that you are currently in is the light's intensity. Light's intensity fluctuates depending on the power of the light source. The camera is able to adjust to the different intensities of light through an adjustable hole in the lens called the iris.

LENS IRIS

When light's intensity is too bright, the **lens iris** (lens aperture) can decrease in size to reduce the light coming into the camera. When the light's intensity is low, the iris can increase in size to allow more light to enter. Does the iris bear any similarity to a human function? If you said yes, it is similar to the human eye, then you are correct. The lens iris and the human eye function in the same way. Low light means big hole; lots of light means small hole. Remember this.

The size of the hole is determined by a number. This number is called an **F-Stop**. The smaller the number, the larger the hole.

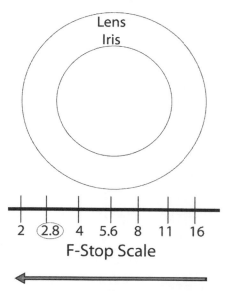

Moving down the scale increases the lens iris.

The larger the number, the smaller the hole. The numbers are represented in this way: 2, 2.8, 4, 5.6, 8, 11, 16, 22, and so on. The starting number and the ending number really depends on the type, quality and power of the lens. What is important to remember is that each number represents a stop. As you move from one stop to the next, the amount of light is either doubled or cut in half. Moving from 2.8 to 2 will double the amount of light entering the lens. Moving from 5.6 to 8 will cut the amount of light coming through the lens in half. How do you know what number to choose? Should you set it to 5.6 or 8? Maybe it's not 8 but 11. How do you know? Well the camera has a few built in features to help you with this potential dilemma. Most cameras have what is called a reflective light meter. The meter reads the light reflected off of objects. Most cameras also have zebra patterns, which work together with the light meter. When more light is reflected the meter reads this and zebra patterns emerge around the areas that are brighter. Reducing the f-stop numbers will cause more

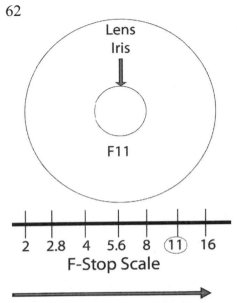

Moving up the scale decreases the lens iris.

light to enter the camera and will also increase the amount of zebra patterns. Remember, zebra patterns detect the amount of light, but they are not recorded in the camera. They will not become part of your image.

We are still missing a piece to manage the image better: a gray card. The reflective light meter reads the amount of light, the zebra patterns detect the amount of light, and the gray card allows for the zebra patterns to detect accurately. So what is so special about a gray card? After all, it's just a gray card. It is not the color that is so important, but the fact that it reflects 18% of the light. This percentage of reflection will give an image good exposure. You only need to see a little bit of zebra patterns on the gray card. Too much could provide an image that is slightly overexposed. To adjust the amount of zebra patterns, use the f-stop scale.

One last note concerning the zebra patterns – on the camera there are usually two settings for them: 70% and 100%. A setting of 70% instructs the camera that the zebra patterns are detecting light reflected off a gray card. (We'll cover one possible use of the 100% setting in just a little bit.) Any photography store carries gray cards from $8.00 to $50.00. The more expensive gray cards are usually waterproof. There are even some gray cards packaged in a collapsible disk.

CAMERA WHITE BALANCE

The second part of light that interests us is its color. Depending on the light source, all light has a color tint to it. The sun has a blue cast to it, household bulbs have an orange cast to them, and a fluorescent tube has a green cast to it. A good question to ask is why does light have color? This is due to what is inside the light. Light is made up of wavelengths. Wavelengths are measured in nanometers (nm). Red has a wavelength of about 700nm and violet has a wavelength of about 400nm. All the other colors fall between these two numbers. These wavelengths are a combination of a complete spectrum of colors. Some light sources have more of one wavelength than another. So the sunlight that you see during the day has more blue wavelength, but the sunlight that you see during the evening has more orange/red wavelengths. House light bulbs have more yellow/orange wavelengths and fluorescent tube lights have more green wavelengths.

In order for a camera to film an object's colors consistently under different light sources, the camera needs to correct for the color tints from the light source. The camera can accomplish this by what is called **white balancing the camera**. Most cameras have presets and custom settings.

The presets are factory-set settings for certain light sources. If you are filming under the sun's light, then set the preset to the sun. If you are filming under your house light bulbs, then set the preset to the light bulb. Most of the presets have icons that

64

are similar to the visual representation of the light source. For example, the fluorescent preset icon looks oblong with little rays around it.

A custom white balance setting allows you to set white balances for light sources for which there is not a preset or if the preset does not quite fit its intended light source. In order to set a custom white balance, you will need a white surface that has adequate brightness. To have accurate brightness on the white surface, use the camera's zebra patterns, but instead of setting them to 70% (which is for the gray card), set them to 100% and adjust the iris to show little zebra patterns on the white surface. Once the light adjustment is complete, the light from the source must illuminate the white surface. Fill the frame completely with the white surface. Then set the white balance to one of its custom settings. There are usually two marked A and B. Just pick one.

Last, you have to initiate the white balance by pressing a button, moving a switch, or flipping a toggle rod. It is different for every camera. If in doubt, check your camera's manual, but one of the three methods given should hit the target. Once you set a custom setting, it is stored in the camera's memory. If you return to that same lighting source, you can easily use the saved white balance setting.

REALLY BRIGHT LIGHT

We already know that the lens iris controls the amount of light entering the camera, but what if we close the iris to its lowest setting, let's say its F11, and there is still too much light entering the lens. What do we do? Do we just leave the image overexposed? Let's switch back to our eyes. What do we do when it is too bright outside? We squint, and when we are tired of squinting we put on sunglasses. The darker the sunglasses are the greater the light reduction.

CAMERA NEUTRAL DENSITY FILTERS

The camera has sunglasses that can reduce the amount of light when the iris is closed to its smallest setting (smallest being F11). These sunglasses are called **neutral density filters** (ND Filters) and there are usually three of them. Each one has different strengths to cut down on the amount of light entering the lens.

We will usually use the ND filters outside during the day. Be mindful that if you move your camera indoors and you find that your image is really dark, you should check to see if the ND filter is not set.

REALLY DIM LIGHT

What if the lens iris is open all the way and we still need more light? What should we do? We could add light, but what if there are no lights to add. We could move to a brighter location, but what if we cannot? What if we are stuck in the location that we are in and there are no lights to add? Do we just film the scene underexposed? Well the manufacturers of cameras are smart individuals. They knew we would run into this problem at some point so they created a way for us to boost the camera's sensitivity to light. When the camera is more sensitive to light it is able to record video under low light. This setting is called the camera Gain.

CAMERA GAIN

There are usually multiple settings for the **Gain** and it is measured in decibels (dB). A setting of 0dB has no gain, but settings of 6dB and 12dB mean the brightness has increased in brightness. There is a trade off that you must log into your memory; after about 12dB the image becomes grainy. Approaching 18dB the image appears really grainy and electronic. This is something you need to watch for because if you do not intend to have a grainy image but you use 18dB, you can be sure your recorded image will be very grainy.

CAMERA SHUTTER

There is a part of the camera that cuts down the amount of light entering the camera like the iris of the lens. It is called the **shutter**. Instead of reducing the iris hole, the shutter blocks the light for a fraction of a second. If you decrease the shutter angle, it will block the light for a longer duration. On the other hand, if you increase the shutter angle, it will block light for a shorter duration.

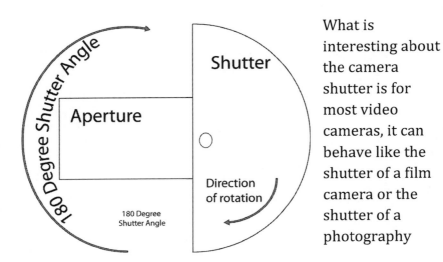

What is interesting about the camera shutter is for most video cameras, it can behave like the shutter of a film camera or the shutter of a photography camera.

Film Camera Shutter

The shutter speed of a film camera is fixed. It has 24 rotations in one second and the shutter angle is 180-degrees. By increasing the size of the shutter this will decrease the shutter angle from 180 to 90, 30 or even 15-degrees. Decreasing the shutter angle gives you a sharper image. It can also give you a staccato look to your image. It is good for action work. Keep in mind that decreasing the shutter angle also decreases the exposure. You will need to decrease the F-Stop or use the Gain to compensate for the light loss.

Photography Camera Shutter

With the photography shutter the speed does change. One frame can get 1/60 of a second of light or 1/250 of a second of light. A film camera shutter is always set to 1/48 of a second. Where it gets interesting is when you slow the photography shutter down below 1/30 of a second. If there is any motion by the camera or within the frame, the image will look slurred. The more you decrease the speed, the greater the slur. This is a cool effect to remember when you need to create a dream sequence or something related. As you reduce the shutter speed, remember to increase the F-Stop because more light is now entering the camera.

You usually have to set the video camera to behave like a film camera or like a photography camera. Most consumer cameras usually have their shutters set to behave like a photography camera. You can see the shutter in operation if you videotape inside under low light. As people walk in front of the camera, they will have that slurred or ghost effect.

68
DISTANCE

Why do some people have to wear glasses? Usually the accuracy of their vision decreases over distance or up close. What is happening within their eye is the image that they are looking at is not correctly falling onto the focus area that is at the back of their eye. When the image falls in front of or behind the focus area of their eye, the image will appear blurry. The further the image is from the focus area, the blurrier the image is to the person. So what is the determining factor for a blurry image? It is the distance. The distance of the objects will determine if they are blurry and how much blurriness they will have. To correct this problem, the person has to wear glasses. The glasses correct the offset of the image from the focus area that is in back of the eye. This is why some people need to wear glasses.

CAMERA FOCUS

Cameras are not much different from the human eye. There is a focus area that is in the camera, and when an image falls in front of or behind this focus area, the image will appear out-of-focus. To correct this we have to make an adjustment to the camera lens so that the image can fall directly on the **focus** area. Shifting the lens forward or backwards does this. This process is called focusing the image. Remember that focusing is based on distance; if your actor moves closer to the camera, you might need to adjust the focus.

I used the words, "might need to adjust the focus," but if the distance changes at all shouldn't we have to adjust the focus? The answer is yes and no. With every focus setting there is an area around that particular distance that still remains in focus.

The distance that is still in focus is called the depth of field, however, the space around the focus setting is not proportional. The space in front of the subject that is toward the camera is only one-third of the distance of the space that remains in focus behind the subject. This depth of field will increase with wide-angle lenses and decrease with long lenses. Also, depth of field will increase at large f-stops (i.e. F11, F16, F22, etc.) and will decrease with small f-stops (i.e. F1.8, F2, F4, etc.).

For all cameras, there is a certain distance at which everything is in focus and this distance is called **infinity**. Where does this infinity start? It starts after the lens' last numeric distance setting. Okay, what does this mean? As you focus the camera, the lens will show us what distance it is now set to, and after the last numeric distance the lens is now set to infinity. An example will clear up any confusion. We are filming a concert that is one hundred feet away from the camera. On the camera there are focus settings from 3 feet to 50 feet. If we set the camera to 51 feet is the concert in focus? The answer is yes because the infinity setting is after the last distance setting, which in this case is 50 – i.e. there really *is* no 51, but rather, the next setting is infinity. To make this even easier, on many professional cameras there is an infinity marking that makes it easy to set.

70

THINKING QUESTIONS

1. If you have two focal lengths one at 25mm and another at 100mm, which one is considered a wide angle and which one is considered telephoto?

2. If the iris is small, is the F-Stop towards the right side of the scale or the left side of the scale?

3. What filter can you use to correct for a situation with really bright light?

4. If you have opened up the iris to its widest setting, does that represent a small F-number or a large F-number?

5. How is focus measured?

CHAPTER EIGHT
IMAGE STABILIZERS

How do we keep the camera steady? The short answer to this question is just set the camera on a steady surface that will keep the camera secure before, during, and after the shot. The long answer is to discuss the many, many support systems for a camera. Now we are not going to go into detail with all the support systems, but I do want to discuss the basic one, which is the tripod.

TRIPOD

A tripod usually attaches itself to the bottom of the camera. Most tripods have what is called a **release plate**. This release plate allows the camera to attach to and detach from the tripod relatively quickly and securely. When using any type of release plate, it is very important to perform a **camera test** after attaching the camera to the tripod. The camera test is simple to

72

perform. Lift the camera by its handle, and the tripod should remain attached and intact. Most tripods have several parts: the legs, the spreader, the head, and the panhandle. Each part serves its own function.

The tripod legs are the major support for the camera. It can have one, two, or three extensions. When using the extensions, always extend the largest portions of the legs first.

The tripod spreader helps keep the tripod legs at equal distance. Sometimes, depending on the situation, it isn't necessary to have the tripod at equal distances and you can use the spreader and adjust it accordingly.

The tripod head allows the camera to tilt, angling up and down, and pan turning the camera left to right. There is a lock and tension control for each movement. The lock tightens the head so it cannot tilt, pan, or both. The tension does not lock the movement, but it only applies a certain amount of pressure. Turning the knob controls the pressure. If tilt or pan is locked, do not try to force a movement. This could ruin the head. Many times, a person will think that the tension is on, but actually the camera is locked. In order to avoid damage to the head, make sure the tilt or pan is unlocked before using the tripod.

The tripod panhandle is the rod that extends from the tripod head, and it is used to pan and tilt the camera. There are two common mistakes to avoid. The first is carrying the tripod by its panhandle. Always carry the tripod by its legs or in a carrying bag. The second mistake is storing the tripod with the head tilted up or down. Locking the head in a tilted position for long periods of time could cause damage to the tripod head.

MONOPODS

A quick way to stabilize a camera is to use a monopod. It is a tripod minus two legs so it only has one. Accordingly, you cannot take your hand off of the monopod. Otherwise, it will fall to the floor. This type of support helps to keep the camera steady and takes the weight off of holding the camera in your hands or on your shoulder. Be mindful of the camera level. Even a little leaning to the left or the right will cause the camera to seem off angle.

OTHER SUPPORT

Do you need to use a tripod? No, but it's a good practice that provides stable support for the camera. Using the camera on the floor is interesting, but the floor can also stabilize the camera. Look for a hard, sturdy surface that is long and wide enough to keep the camera safe. With this in mind, you might consider using a table, stool, chair, a counter, desk, a car hood or even your lap. In high traffic areas with people walking to and fro, always keep a hand on the camera to minimize any accidents and prevent any thefts.

THINKING QUESTIONS

1. What is a release plate? How does it help you speed up productivity?

2. How is a monopod different from a tripod? In what situations might a monopod be more useful than a tripod?

3. What is a camera test?

CHAPTER NINE
IMAGE QUALITY

There are four major factors to consider when thinking about the quality of an image: the lens, the resolution, the frames per second (fps), and the exhibition. The lens and the resolution are the usual marketing features for selling a camera. What is not used very often is the exhibition because it focuses on how an image is seen. Let's look at each factor individually.

LENS

The camera **lens** is the entry point for any image to enter the camera. Think of it as a tunnel and some tunnels are cleaner than others. Some tunnels cost more to build while others are cleaned on a regular basis. Other tunnels are built with materials that allow them to last for years and years. Just like a tunnel, a lens also has many properties that affect the quality of the image. The main determining factors are as follows:

1. The quality of glass used to make the lens.
2. The housing that holds the glass.
3. Whether the lens is a prime (one focal length) or zoom (multiple focal lengths). Usually a prime lens provides a sharper image than a zoom lens. This is due to the image traveling through less glass. A zoom lens has more glass to travel through than a prime lens.

RESOLUTION

The **resolution** of the image states how much information the image can hold. A frame defines each image. For instance, a 35mm film area places the image within a 35mm frame. Video cameras can have multiple resolution settings that you can manipulate. The higher the resolution, the more information an image can hold. So what does this mean? It means that if you recorded the same image at different resolutions, the image with the higher resolution will have captured more information from the same image. By using a camera with high resolution, you are able to see the pores of someone's skin, but on a camera with low resolution, the pores are not even visible. The higher resolution image records more information, which in this case are the pores on someone's face.

High Definition images (HD) have resolutions of 1440x1080i, that is 1,440 pixels across by 1,080 pixels down. The "i" at the end stands for interlace. An interlaced image means that the image is broken up into two. These are called fields. The first field has all of the odd numbered pixels. The second field has all of the even numbered pixels. The odd numbered pixels are shown first.

76

Another type of HD resolution does not have fields; this resolution is 960x720, and because this resolution has no fields, it is called progressive. Progressive means that each frame has exactly 960x720 pixels. Lower resolution images are considered standard definition (SD). This resolution is 720x480.

How do you choose the right resolution? To some it is just easier to film everything in HD. The more the merrier, right? Maybe, but not always. HD requires a lot of space to store information and a strong processor in order to view your footage. It is always best to have a 500 GB or 1 TB external drive available when filming large projects. Prices are constantly falling on storage media, so check your local electronics store and look for sales. Small projects of 5 minutes or less are okay to put on your computer's hard drive, but remember that multiple 5-minute projects can add up quickly. When selecting the best resolution to use, it is better to think of how your audience will view your project. Will viewing take place in a theater? If so, go with the highest resolution you can afford. If you'll be broadcasting on a two inch by 3-inch space on someone's computer monitor, then it is okay to film at SD.

FRAMES PER SECOND (FPS)

How do we get motion? Motion is achieved by a bunch of pictures passing by your eyes so fast that your brain thinks it's motion. This brain trick is called **persistence of vision**. When that first image appears on screen, it is there for a split second, then the next image appears. The first image still remains in your mind very, very briefly, but just briefly enough to blend into the second image. The number of frames is broken down by seconds. Film shows 24 pictures every second. Another way to say it is 24 **frames per second** (fps). Most video cameras can also show 24fps. Traditional fps is 30. A growing standard for video is to use 60 fps. The more fps, the sharper the image.

Using fps and resolution looks like this: 1440x1080, 30i or 960x720, 24p. The 1440x1080 is the resolution and the 30i is the frames per second and the "I" means that there are two fields for each frame. So there are a total of 60 fields for the 30 frames.

FAST/SLOW MOTION

How do we get slow motion or fast motion? If the frames per second give us motion, how do we change the fps to achieve a slower or faster motion? If we slow down the number of frames per second while recording and playing the images back at a normal speed, then we will have fast motion. For example, what if we change the fps from 24 to 12 then record a person running? When we play back the sequence the person will move twice as fast. Conversely, what if we increase the fps from 24 to 60 then record a person running? When we play it back, the person will move two and a half times slower.

EXHIBITION

Will a film be viewed in a theater, on a television screen, a plasma screen, or on a small section of the computer? Take all of this into account when you are choosing the resolution for your project. You should use HD if the project will be on the big screen, but SD will do if it's showing on television or on a computer screen. I guess what I really want to stress is that you do not have to film on the highest resolution just because

78

it's available to you. Think about your end result. How will the audience view your piece of work? Then plan accordingly.

Let's quickly discuss a problem that a smaller resolution could fix. Let's say that you filmed a project and all the footage was slightly soft or slightly out of focus. If you play the project at its normal resolution, it will look slightly out of focus. BUT if you scale it down to 70% or less, the image will appear sharper. So in this case, smaller is better.

THINKING QUESTIONS

1. What are the four major factors to think about when it comes to image quality?

2. Why is resolution important? When is using a low resolution appropriate?

3. How does the camera lens determine image quality?

4. What steps could you take to improve the quality of your film?

CHAPTER TEN
AUDIO

MAINTAINING 100%

Can anything in the film achieve 100%? The audio should get as close as possible. Every film has flaws, but this is not true for audio. Audio is the one part of your film that must maintain 100% (give or take a few percentage points). What does this mean? It means that the recorded audio has to have high quality. Most people are more forgiving of the visual image than the auditory sound. This is due to the emotional connection that sound brings to film. It is said that film is 70% information and 30% emotional, but sound is 70% emotional and 30% information. When flaws and low quality disturb that connection the audience immediately notices a difference. Our aim is to constantly keep the audience engaged and connected to the film. We do this by aiming for the highest audio standard possible.

AUDIO METERS

What measures the audio? Most cameras have a way to view the measurement of the audio and this measurement is taken through the **audiometers**. When the microphone picks up sound, it will have a visual representation. This visual representation is indicated by a fluctuating bar or line within your camera. Inside the computer, the audio is represented by fluctuating waves called **audio waveforms**.

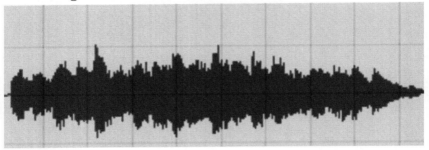

When zooming into the waveform, we can see the individual waves. The height of the wave is the loudness of the sound. This is called the **amplitude**. Most sounds heard in everyday life have fluctuating amplitudes, which is a change in the height of the wave. Inside the camera, the height of the wave is represented

by a bar or line. A low wave will have a short bar, but a high wave or loud sound will have a taller bar. What you have to remember is the loudest sound cannot rise or extend into the red or over 0.

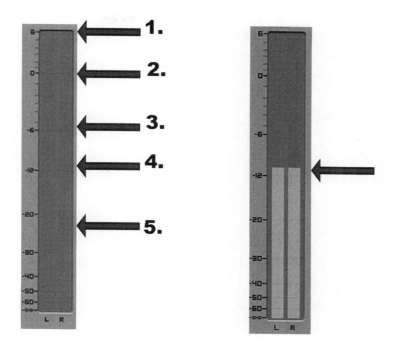

In the above image, the scale on the left points out different areas of the audio scale. If the highest point of the audio fluctuates to the number 5 arrow, then your audio is recording too low. To resolve this problem increase the volume control for the microphone and/or move the microphone closer to the source.

If the highest point of the audio is fluctuating between the numbers 3 and 4, this is great. This is about two thirds to three fourths up the scale and gives room for the audio to increase without causing errors (going over 0).

82

Having the audio rise to number 2 is too close and you can blow the audio, which is an audio error. It is best to lower the audio control for the microphone to solve this problem. It is not necessary to move the microphone further from the source because you want the audio to sound as crisp and clean as possible.

When the audio extends over 0 and into the area marked with number 1, the audio is unusable. Usually the bar that registers the audio inside of the camera will change to red to inform you when you are approaching 0 or if you are over 0. In either case, back off the audio by reducing the volume.

Sometimes it is very appropriate to **ride the audio**. This means you will have to adjust the audio, slightly shifting it higher and lower, to achieve good recording. This takes a little practice, but after a while, it becomes second nature.

If we look at the waveform from the previous page, we can see that the curves are made up of dots. These dots are called **samples**. They are the recorded information from the actual sound. Audio for video records 48,000 samples per second or 48kHz. CD audio records at 44,100 samples per second or 44.1kHz.

RECORDING AMBIENCE

It is always a good, no, a *great* idea to record the ambience of a room before leaving the location. The ambience of a room is the noise in the room that you can hear when no one is moving or speaking. The wind blowing against the windowpane, the refrigerator motor, or a computer CPU are all examples of items that will make up the ambience of a room. Sometimes there aren't any of these types of items and the ambience is only the air that is moving through the room. Using the recorded ambience for sequential clips will greatly help smooth the audio in the editing process.

When recording dialogue it's important to have your dialogue audio level higher than your ambient audio level. Your dialogue should record about -16 to -12 and your ambience around -24, -30 or even lower, if possible. The closer you can get the microphone to your actors speaking, the better your audio will record.

THINKING QUESTIONS

1. What does 100% Audio mean?

2. What is a good level for audio recording?

3. Why is it important to record ambience?

4. What are some good steps to take while recording audio?

CHAPTER ELEVEN
PUTTING IT ALL TOGETHER

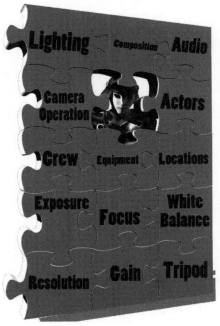

It's easy to read about techniques and procedures in books, magazines, and on the Internet. Taking the information and using it is a different story. Filming outside or inside requires a certain understanding of different functions of the camera and the challenges that come with the environment or setting.

FILMING OUTSIDE ON A SUNNY DAY

Filming outside has it pluses and minuses. The plus is the available light. The minus is controlling the available light and the noise. Follow these necessary steps to improve your chances of success while filming outdoors.

1. **White Balance.** Set your camera's White Balance to the "Sun" preset or set a custom White Balance. Remember to completely fill the frame with something that is white if taking a custom White Balance. Don't forget to set your Zebra Patterns to 100%.

2. **Gain.** Make sure your camera's gain is **off**.

3. **Exposure.** Adjust your exposure to around 8 or 11 or toward the end of your F-Stop scale. Use a Gray Card for accurate exposure. Make sure you set your Zebra Patterns to 70%.

4. **ND Filter.** You might need to use your Camera's sunglasses.

5. **Sun.** Place your Talent at an angle to the sun, but try not to film with the sun directly behind them or the camera operator. If the sun is directly behind them it can cause lens flare and any dust on the lens is immediately noticeable.

6. **Reflector.** Use a reflector to bounce the sunrays into the shadows. A reflector is great to minimize shadows on faces.

7. **Microphone.**

     a. If you are only using the on-camera microphone, then keep your talent 2 to 3 feet from the camera. Keep the camera pointed toward the talent's face to clearly pick up their dialogue.

86

8. If it's windy, use anything you can find to block the wind from hitting the microphone. You can have one or two individuals stand on the sides of the camera or whichever direction the wind is blowing from.

9. **COMPOSITION.**

   a. Focus on using a Master Shot versus breaking up the scene into multiple shots.

   b. If using a Master Shot, cover yourself by filming adequate cut-a-ways.

   c. Don't forget to film other objects, items, or elements of your scene beside the talent (i.e. the sky, the cars, the buildings, the trees, the leaves, the grass, etc.)

10. **FILMING.**

    a. Use a Slate and write the scene number and take.

    b. Film at least two good takes.

    c. Let the camera run for at least 3 seconds before you call "action" and 3 seconds after you call "cut." Having this extra room is very helpful with editing when you want to add a transition.

    d. Use a shot list to keep track of what shots are needed and what shots are still not completed.

FILMING OUTSIDE ON A CLOUDY DAY

Filming outside on a cloudy day has an additional benefit over filming on a sunny day. The clouds help give an even, diffused light. The sun illuminates the entire area.

1. **White Balance.** It is better to use a custom White Balance versus using the sun preset. This is due to the rise in color temperature on cloudy days. Don't forget to fill the frame with something white and set the Zebra

Patterns to 100%. Showing just a sprinkle of Zebra Patterns is okay. The Zebra Patterns do not need to cover the entire surface.

2. **Gain.** Make sure it is off.
3. **ND Filter.** After adjusting the exposure you might need to use the ND filters to cut down more light entering the camera.
4. **Reflector.** Even though the light is diffused you can still use a reflector, especially to fill in the eye sockets with a little light.
5. See steps 7 – 9 from the ***Sunny Day*** section.

FILMING OUTSIDE AT NIGHT

Filming outside at night raises more lighting challenges than anything else, but with a little creativity, you can still pull off a great scene. What to remember is to rethink how you use light.

1. **White Balance.** Will you be using any of the camera presets? Set a custom White Balance. See the notes in the above sections about the Custom White Balance.
2. **Location.** Location is key when filming outside at night. Select a location that has multiple streetlights or houses that utilize their porch lights.
3. **Gain.** You may or may not need the gain, but if you are trying to raise the light levels of the entire area, set your gain to about 12db. Remember: high numbers of gain (i.e. 18db) will generate a grainy image.
4. **Lighting.**
   a. What about filming your talent in silhouette? Is it really necessary to show their faces? Think of all the films and comic books you have seen that use this technique. Just place your subject in front of

the light. For example, if using a porch light, place your talent in the yard so you can see the light on both sides of the talent.

    b. What about using a car's headlights to light your talent or provide a silhouette of your talent?

    c. Use a flashlight or multiple flashlights. To keep them stationary, tape them to broomsticks, chairs, stools, etc. One thing to note is that most flashlights produce rings of light. Be mindful of this. You might not want this effect on your scene or against your talent.

5. See steps 7-9 from the **Sunny Day** section.

FILMING INSIDE A HOUSE

Filming inside will allow you to have greater control over the lighting and sound. The downside to filming inside is the amount of time needed to make the necessary adjustments. Remember to give yourself adequate time to set the lights and/or remove unwanted sounds from the scene. Think with your eyes as well as your ears.

1. **White Balance.** If you are using regular household bulbs, you can use the light bulb preset. Even when using the preset, the scene will have a slight orange tint. This is due to the fact that normal household bulbs have a lower color temperature than the preset of your camera. If this is unwanted, use a Custom White Balance. See the notes from above on setting the Custom White Balance.

2. **Windows.** Are you going to use the window light with the household bulbs? If you decide to do this, just remember that you are mixing color temperatures. If your camera is balanced to the household bulbs, then the light coming from the windows will appear blue. If you balance for the window light, the light from the household bulbs will appear orange. To solve this color temperature problem, close the curtains and use only the household bulbs or turn off the household bulbs and only use the light from the windows. A second solution is to color correct the household bulbs by placing conversion gels around the light. Don't place the conversion gel on the light bulb. The bulb will burn the gel. A third solution is to swap the household bulbs out for photo bulbs. The photo bulbs are color balanced to match the sun's color temperature. See your local photography store for photo bulbs.

3. **Reflector.** Use a reflector to bounce the light from whatever source you are using to fill shadow areas.

4. **Light.** Remember you can use the shadows created by the lights to help tell your story.

5. **Sound.** If possible, unplug any noisy refrigerators, heaters or other distracting sounds. Close windows if sounds from the outside are noticeable. Have the crew take off their shoes if walking noises are too loud or noticeable.

6. **Microphone.** If you are only using the on-camera microphone, keep your talent 2 to 3 feet from the camera. Keep the camera pointed toward the talent's face to clearly pick up their dialogue.

90

7. **Composition.** Add additional shots that repeat the action from the Master Shot, but cover the action from a different angle and/or different shot size.

8. See step 9 from the ***Sunny Day*** section.

FILMING INSIDE A SCHOOL

One thing to note when filming inside a school is the need for a custom white balance because more than likely, all of the lights are fluorescent. Most video cameras do not have a preset for fluorescent lights. Many photography cameras do, but sometimes it takes more time to select the best one then it would take to just do a custom white balance. See steps 2 – 8 for Filming Inside a House for other helpful steps.

THINKING QUESTIONS

1. When filming outside during the day, how should you set your white balance?

2. When filming inside, how would your exposure differ from filming outside during the day?

3. What are some lighting concerns to think about when filming at night?

4. How does white balance differ from filming inside a house versus filming inside a school?

5. What are the differences between filming on a cloudy day and filming on a sunny day?

CHAPTER TWELVE
EDITING

There is an essential step that involves putting your clips together for the audience to view. This process is called editing. Editing can take anywhere from a few minutes to a few years. This depends on the complexity of putting the clips together, which can determine how much time is spent. An easy edit will only require a short time, but a difficult edit will have you sitting down with your editing software for a long, long time, and that's okay. Whatever it takes to get it done. Even though the goal is to aim for a great edit, at some point you will have to come to an end. You can always find something within your project that you can do better. We all can, but it is important to finish it to the best of your abilities and move forward.

BACK UP

It's very easy to lose a project and all related clips. This is why it is important to **back up** your clips. Currently DVDs can store up to 8.5GB (gigabytes). If you are filming at 1440x1080i then you will need 1GB for every minute. If you have a 3-minute film at a 4:1 shooting ratio then you will need 12GB of storage or 2 DVDs that hold 8.5GB each. A 5 pack of DVDs will cost about $13.00 at an office supply store. You can also save copies of your project file on a USB drive (flash drive or jump drive).

EDITING AT THE SAME RESOLUTION

The resolution that your camera was set to is the same resolution to edit on the computer. If you filmed at 1080i at 30 fps, then you should edit at 1080i at 30 fps. If you are unsure what setting your camera was on, just check your camera menu settings. Match the resolution and frame rate.

MANAGING THE EDIT

Have you ever tried purchasing an item at a store you are unfamiliar with? You know what you want, you know what the item looks like, and you even know about where it is located. Even when you know all of this, it takes time to find the item because you are unfamiliar with the store. What valuable commodity is affected? It is your time. The more familiar you are, the faster you are able to move to get what you need. Editing is the same way. You know the footage you filmed, but finding the shots you want is a time intensive process UNLESS you manage the footage first.

Management will get you to the finish line faster. The first step is to organize your footage into some basic categories as follows:

1. One for Audio
2. One for Video
3. One for images

Any recorded audio files will go under the audio category and images that you might create in Photoshop, Illustrator or that you have taken with your camera will go under the image category.

Another good idea is to create a few other categories within your main categories. This is an especially good idea for the video section. You can organize your video clips by similarities. This way you can access them quickly. For the audio you can create subcategories for sound effects, voiceovers, music, and ambience.

The last part of management is naming your clips and providing detailed information about each one using the clips' available reference fields. It is helpful to catalog your files precisely so they're easy to find when you need them. Keep in mind the more video clips you have, the better you need to manage them. If you only have one or two clips, you do not have to do much at all because knowing what is in two clips is pretty easy. It's when you get to ten, twenty, or thirty clips that you need to practice good management techniques.

EDIT TO SCRIPT & STORYBOARD

So how do you start editing your clips together? Edit to your script. The script will tell you how much of a clip to use and how often to use it. The storyboard and floor plan will tell you what type of clip to use when you have multiple clips with the same content but different shot sizes and angles.

EDITING OUT THE BAD STUFF

The goal is for the finished film to look as good as possible, so it is important to edit out any mistakes, flaws, or problems you had during filming. If the entire clip is a flaw don't use it. Find a clip that really represents your story.

SELECTING THE BEST MATERIAL

What if you have multiple takes with no flaws? At this point it is important to watch your footage. Watch it over and over again. Go get some orange juice, milk, water, or some good punch to sip on as you watch your clips. Pay close attention to the details – how the camera moves, how the actor's head moves, etc. The different facial reactions and body movements are very important and will vary from take to take. Pick one that best represents the story and edit it into the rough cut.

USING CUTS ONLY

With all the dissolves and transitions, the best method to use for joining clips together is the cut. The cut is simple. It is placing one clip next to another. Use dissolves when showing an elapse in time. An example is going from nighttime to the morning. Other transitions are used to give specific meaning. For example, you might use a certain effect to enter a dream and return from the dream. As a rule, use transitions sparingly.

Avoid using many different transitions within a project because your project can start to look gaudy.

MATCHED EDITING

Matched Editing is editing two clips together during a movement. For example, if an actor was framed in a Long Shot and the actor started to raise her arm, you would end the first clip when the arm is about halfway in the air. Then you would find the Medium Shot of the actor raising her arm but start the clip with the arm already halfway in the air. It is important to look at the angle of the arm from the Medium Shot to the Long Shot and match the angle from one clip to the next precisely. By adhering to this process, you will have completed an invisible edit.

Use Matched Editing when you have any action within your scene. Especially use it for fight scenes and chase scenes. You will find that using this technique will bring slickness to your edits and overall project presentation.

OVERLAPPING EDITING (J Cut/L Cut)

To help improve the illusion of edits, it is important to use overlapping editing. This technique helps to pull the audience from one clip to the next. It is accomplished by either introducing the audio of a clip edit before the video appears or by introducing the video edit before the audio is heard. Let's say you have a clip of a car passing. Having the audio edit occur before the video, the audience will hear the car passing a second or two before the audience actually sees the car. This is a J Cut. Let's say there is a conversation between two people and the audience sees the reaction of the one who is not

96

speaking for few seconds, then the actor begins speaking. The part of the clip that shows the reaction is the video starting before the audio. This is an L Cut.

STARTING FROM BLACK/ENDING IN BLACK

How do you represent a beginning and ending? You can fade from black to begin your story and fade to black to end it. It's like being in a dark theater. It is dark to help focus the viewers' attention on what is important, which is the film projected on the screen. Also when you wake up, you open your eyes then begin your day. At the end of the day you close your eyes again. Editing from black at the beginning and to black at the end falls in line with how we conduct our daily lives. Many films you watch will also fade from black and at the end return to black. This is a simple technique but very effective.

USING TITLES/CREDITS

Since you are using black at the beginning, what would be the most effective color to use for your **titles** and **credits**? If you said white, you are correct. White titles provide a good contrast to a black background and they really make a statement. When you are typing your titles, be mindful of the useful guides that keep the text within the boundaries. Keeping your text inside the guides allow it to safely play on different monitors and projectors without cropping the Titles.

MAKING CORRECTIONS

There are usually two types of corrections that most editing programs allow you to adjust – the brightness and color of your clips. These adjustments are not for visual effects but for correcting clips that were a little too overexposed (too bright) and slightly off the white balance. Find these two correction filters within your software and adjust certain clips when necessary.

THINKING QUESTIONS

1. How can you back up your project? What media can you use to accomplish it?

2. Why is it important to use the title guides when creating titles and credits?

3. Why is the CUT edit so effective?

4. Give a couple reasons why using black at the beginning and end of your film is important.

5. What corrections could you consider using when you complete your edit?

CHAPTER THIRTEEN
SOUNDTRACK

What do you think drives the emotion of a film? Usually it is the sound. Images provide the information, but the sound drives the emotion. It's important to spend enough time developing the sound of the film so that it helps enhance the story.

DIALOGUE

It's important to keep the **dialogue** of each cut at the same audio levels. You might have to adjust the individual tracks to keep the dialogue tracks consistent. Keep the highest point of the dialogue at the ¾ mark of the audiometers. Use a 3 to 6 frame audio transition from one clip to the next to help blend the audio between clips.

AMBIENT TRACK

Use the ambient clip that you recorded during filming across the entire scene. Adjust the ambient level to the ¼ mark of the audiometers. The **ambient track** will help smooth the audio from one clip to the next. If the ambient clip is not long enough to cover the entire scene, use it again and again until you reach the end of the scene. Remember: as the location changes, so should the ambience for that particular location.

SOUND DESIGN

Hearing birds flying, dogs barking, cars passing, doors unlocking, footsteps moving, children laughing, etc., are all part of the **sound design** of the film. These sounds help bring life to your story and give it a certain feeling. If a scene includes arguing between characters, use sounds that can help those visuals.

EFFECTS

The audio **effects** give audio impact to certain visuals. It might be the sound of a chair falling or a baseball hitting the glove. Effects are always tied to something visual.

SCORE

The piano playing softly as an actor walks up the stairs is part of the **sound score**. The score includes those instruments playing to enhance the viewers' experience. When there is fear, there is music to enhance the fear. When there is action, instruments accompany it. Take careful consideration when selecting instruments for a score. It is not necessary or even desirable to have the score play for the duration of the film – just during moments when the enhancement is warranted.

100

MUSIC

What about that song that you long to hear on the radio? Can you just throw it into your project? Besides the copyright infringement issue, the song by your favorite music group might not fit your story. It sounds great to you on your iPod and in the car, but could prove to work against you if the lyrics and rhythm do not match or reinforce your story. If you have to use music, use it sparingly.

For the Sound Design, Effects, Score, and Music, the audio levels will vary in importance. You will need to put them all in place and make necessary adjustments as they are playing.

Remember to add small 4 to 6 frame audio transitions to the beginning and ending of each sound so it does not pop in, but rather, enters the scene smoothly.

Thinking Questions

1. What benefits does a soundtrack provide a film?

2. Why should you use audio transitions between two audio clips?

3. What is a sound design? How is it different than audio effects?

4. Why is it important to use original music?

5. What is a music score and how is it different from a song?

CHAPTER FOURTEEN
EXHIBITION

Once the project is complete, you need to export it and then find ways to exhibit it. The exhibition of a film describes how people will view your film.

EXPORTING THE PROJECT

How many types of exports are there? The short answer is many, but usually all editing platforms provide export formats for normal viewing such as DVD, iPod, YouTube and Internet Streaming. When there is an export to different formats, the resolution of your film can change, so check the export settings.

PROJECT EXHIBITION

With today's technology, there are many avenues to show your film – normal viewing, using a projector, showing your film to a crowd, or placing your film on your iPod are only a few of the options available to you. Technology has changed the way we view media and you can use this to your advantage.

SOCIAL NETWORKS

Most of the social networks you are likely involved in, such as Facebook, have a video component that allows you to upload video. Once it is added, you can invite your friends to watch it and give you comments.

ONLINE VIDEO PROVIDERS

Once you finish your project, it's easy to upload it to YouTube at www.youtube.com. Since your project is short, you can upload it with the settings you used to edit it and YouTube will do the necessary converting. Another free service that is similar to YouTube, but dedicated to artists, is Vimeo. You can find it at www.vimeo.com. A student video provider is SchoolTube and you can locate them at www.schooltube.com. All three of these video providers have mechanisms to comment on the videos posted.

WITHOUT A BOX

A great free service is WithoutABox. It will help you submit your project to different film festivals and help you with marketing. You can find it at www.withoutabox.com.

THINKING QUESTIONS

1. How do you plan to enable audiences to watch your film?

2. What are some steps you can take to increase the number of viewers who can review your work?

3. Name some online video providers that you are using or plan to use.

4. Visit withoutabox.com. How does this site help your project?

CHAPTER FIFTEEN
CLOSING ADVICE

PRACTICE, PRACTICE, PRACTICE

Once you have finished your first, second, or third film, guess what? It's time to start another one. You can never practice too much. Always have two stories in your head, one you are writing and one you are filming. The more you write, compose, work with actors, edit, and receive constructive criticism, the better filmmaker you will become. Practice makes perfect, so perfectly you must practice.

BUILD RELATIONSHIPS

No one can make it alone. Filmmaking is like any other business, industry, or art form. There is a web of individuals whom are all interconnected to bring about a successful film for viewers to see everyday. It is best to build relationships with people who like to tell the same kind of stories as you do. You will find that working with others will help ease the burden of bringing projects to fruition. Remember, the more you work with professionals and people who are experts within their field, the more quality opinions you will receive. Listen to them all, but only use a few. Incorporating too many different opinions into your story could throw your story off from its original intent.

LEARN MORE

There are hundreds and hundreds of books and magazines and thousands upon thousands of Internet articles along with blogs and videos dedicated to different aspects of filmmaking. Try to learn something new everyday. This is easy to do by subscribing to a few blogs or receiving a few online subscriptions. Five to ten minutes of reading can provide you with many new facts, methods, and processes for filmmaking. Try to read one book a month. Just check with your local library. You will be amazed at the amount of resources they have for you to check out.

106

THANK YOU

It is always a pleasure to educate and provide information. I hope this book has helped you increase your filmmaking skills. I want to thank you for reading and using this content within your projects. Stay in touch through B-South.com. I look forward to viewing your future work.

Suggested Resources

A Fun Book To Read in a Hour!
Shulman and Krog. *Attack of The Killer Video Book: Tips & Tricks For Young Directors.* Annick Press, 2004.

<u>Beef Up Your Knowledge</u>
Proferes, Nicholas. **Film Directing Fundamentals: See Your Film Before Shooting. Focal Press, 2008.**

Brown, Blain. Cinematography: Theory & Practice, Image Making for Cinematographers, Directors and Videographers. Focal Press, 2002

Malkiewicz, Kris. *Cinematography: The Classic Guide to Filmmaking, Revised and Updated for the 21st Century*, 3rd ed. Simon & Schuster, 2005.

<u>A Good Reference Book</u>
Ascher, Steven and Pincus. *The Filmmaker's Handbook: A Comprehensive Guide for the Digital Age.* A Plume Book, 2007.

<u>Will help with your writing.</u>
Armer, Alana A. *Writing The Screenplay: TV and Film*, 2nd ed. Wadsworth, 1993.

<u>To Increase Your Learning</u>
www.b-south.com

<u>To Learn Software Faster</u>
www.lynda.com

108
www.vtc.com

To increase your network
www.ifp.org

Create your website
www.weeby.com

Vocabulary to Memorize

1. **Premise** – A summary of your story in two to three sentences.

2. **Treatment** – An elaboration of your story with all the details about characters, locations, and plots and can even include character background information.

3. **Screenplay** – Your story written in a structured format. Usually one page is one on-screen minute.

4. **Dialogue** – Words that are spoken in a film.

5. **Rewrite** – The process of tweaking the screenplay after it is finished. Making improvements to the plot, characters and dialogue.

6. **Rehearsal** – Time spent reviewing the screenplay with the actors and crew prior to filming. Practicing actor performance and directing before filming.

7. **Composition** – How contents are arranged in the frame for the purpose of filming.

8. **Master Shot** – A take that continues for the duration of the scene filming all the important parts for that scene.

9. **Storyboard** – Still pictures that represent the intended camera set up for the story.

10. **Floor Plan**– A bird's-eye view of camera and actor placement and movement.

11. **Stand In** – A person who stands in for an actor during lighting set-ups.

12. **Shot List**– A written or typed ordered sequence of camera set-ups describing shot size and frame contents.

13. **Crew** – Team members that are responsible for the technical production of the story.

14. **Props** – Items actors will handle during a scene.

15. **Pan** – The camera turns on its axis left or right.

16. **Tilt** –The camera turns on its axis up or down.

17. **Rule Of Thirds** – Method for arranging contents within the frame.

18. **Framing** – Selecting what to record and how to record the selection.

19. **Profile Shot**– Framing a person from the side.

20. **Over-The-Shoulder** – Framing someone over another person's shoulder.

21. **Reaction Shot** – Framing what someone responds to.

22. **Perspective** – Framing that shows three-dimensional space.

23. **Screen Space** - Area in the frame that offsets a person's looking, walking or standing space.

24. **180-Degree Rule** – Rule that maintain camera placement to keep screen direction consistent.

25. **Focal Length** – The magnification of a lens.

26. **Lens Iris–** also the lens aperture is a fluctuating hole that regulates how much light enters the camera.

27. **F-Stop** – The scale that determines how large the diameter of the lens iris is.

28. **White Balance–** Adjusting the camera's colors to match the color of the light.

29. **Neutral Density Filters** – Reduces the intensity of light.

30. **Gain** – Increases the sensitivity of the camera recording pixels.

31. **Shutter** – Interrupts the light from impacting the camera pixels for a set amount of time.

32. **Focus** – The sharpness of an image.

33. **Tripod** – Stabilizing the camera.

34. **Camera Lens** - The part of the camera that allows the image to enter the camera.

35. **Resolution** – The amount of pixels available to capture the image.

36. **Frames Per Second (FPS)** – The number of images recorded each second by the camera.

37. **Audio Meters** – The scale the measures the loudness of sound.

38. **Audio Waveforms** – The visual representation of audio.

39. **Ambience** – The available sound in any given location. The sounds that are created by the environment.

NOTES

Printed in Great Britain
by Amazon.co.uk, Ltd.,
Marston Gate.